FEARLESS

DAYONE Series

Nira Minniefield

published by collective thoughts press, new york.

dedication

This book is dedicated to my children: Jaedon, Kieran and Neysa; you save my life on a daily basis. When I'm with you, I'm home — wherever we are.

To my Mother, the original fearless woman, you are more than you can imagine.

To my sister, I hope you always hold my hand - not because I'm afraid; but because it's always more beautiful when you're around.

To my Father, thank you for the tools: the key, the sword, the flame, the map, the compass. Without them this would not be possible.

To my brother, I believe in you. Always have.

I love you all profoundly.

about

the power of day one.

"Just for today, I will try to live through this day only, and not tackle my whole life problem at once."

-Kenneth L. Holmes

The first day of any new thing is exhilarating. You're jazzed and ready to go. You are poised for striking and certain you can complete whatever is it you are setting out to do: Lose weight, wake up earlier, get that certification or learn a new language...

Midway through, you're second-guessing or have become discouraged. If you are curious, I'll tell you what I've learned:

Just start with today.

If you start by doing one simple thing differently each day, at the end of the year you've built a mountain.

The DAYONE series, gives you 'big subjects' in a short format that you can put to immediate and practical use in one day. The power is in the knowing. Once we know, we can choose true action, less re-action and stay closer to the truth about ourselves on those days when the whirlwind comes and life seems like it is falling down around us.

Welcome to day one.

In this DAYONE book, we'll understand and appreciate FEARLESSNESS.

fearless: table of contents

extra

foreword

My introduction to Nira came in 2012 through her dad - my dear friend Ray Minniefield. Ray has a beautiful, honest soul that wraps you in warmth the minute you meet him, "it don't take a whole day to recognize sunshine".

Soon after we met he said to me, "You have to meet my daughter Nira, the two of you are locked on that same creative wavelength." Later that evening I met Nira the intellectual, over a lively political and socio-economic discourse. As time went on I got to know Nira, the artist and finally Nira, the writer.

If you've never had the pleasure of reading her poetry, seeing her at an open mic or hearing her rock out with a live band – she is engaging, honest and real. Reading her work brings you into her world, and opens you up to a region of mind that is a visceral experience for anyone brave enough to dare go there.

I was fortunate enough to get my hands on a draft copy of "Fearless" and it blew me away. I remember reading it in my office and being stunned by the natural poetry that comes out in her writing with so little effort. This is that "IT" thing which is so often searched for. This isn't crazy talk, this is serious business. People can use this book.

Nira has her finger on the pulse. "We have no need to be so foolishly afraid of what we truly are."

"Fearless" lets us know that we have choices in what we put up with and how we talk to ourselves. What I love about "Fearless" is that it's written in a language easily understood. It screams the FDR quote "there is nothing to fear but fear itself".

Enjoy this gift, and as my dear friend Ray said to me about his daughter

"I'm glad you are seeing what I have seen since she was a baby."

-Keith Thompson

section i.
who are you

1: what is your name

"Let the weak man say, I am strong."

— Joel 3:10, The Bible

This book is a primer on the art of fearless living. It will not tell you the secret combination of things that go into your "Happily Ever After" sauce, that's something only you know and will know more intimately through the principles introduced here.

Let's correct the errors we've taught ourselves about what is and is not possible. Let's identify the sources of these hurt-stories and rewrite those scripts. Let's remember our true name and slay the shadow monsters that have kept us in the margins for so long. Let's learn what goes in the personal power toolbox, and then teach each other how to keep it stocked with everything we need to keep our fire alive.

This book is built like a compass. It will point you in the direction of your own natural greatness and reveal the unlimited personal power you took in with your first breath. With a renewed understanding of yourself, you'll be on the golden road to a life experience we will all stand in awe of.

Your ability to be fearless will serve you well. It will enable you to see clearly and use that laser-like focus to always bring the right combination of people and circumstances into your life. Fearlessness brings us the courage to ACT when those perfect conditions present themselves. It allows us to simplify our lives by worrying less on things that don't deserve our attention and ACTING more on the things that matter most.

In reading this you'll identify the individual aspects of the "Life of Your Dreams". You'll identify those aspects and then you'll finally give yourself permission to actively engage the field of limitless experiences and innumerable possibilities.

The excuses; the hurt-place storytelling and broken mental records are not on your side. You can check those bags at the door.

Ready?

Ok.

Wait!

Hear that?

Your TRUE SELF is already thanking you, and just rose to give you a standing ovation.

Wow.

You're good.

2: what are you so afraid of

"I will face my fear. I will permit it to pass over me
and through me. And when it has gone past...there
will be nothing, only I will remain."
– Frank Herbert Dune

fear /fi(ə)r/
Noun

**An unpleasant emotion caused by the belief that
someone or something is dangerous, likely to
cause pain, or a threat.**

Depending on who you ask, we are currently living
in the "Last Days", a time of "Climate Upheaval",
the "End of the Mayan Calendar" see: Last Days,
"Economic Crisis" and on...

While humanity has seen disaster — from that
pesky Black Plague to The Great Depression —
these days we're subjected to disaster on a daily
basis in an endless play-by-play. News channels,
RSS Feeds, Twitter Notifications, Facebook Updates,
Youtube videos... constant streams of not-always-
good news information.

With so many things competing for our attention, it's a wonder we come out of our houses at all and no wonder that when we do — we do things like flip each other 'the bird' in a moment of road rage or kick-box each other in a department store over a large tv on 'Black Friday'.

In the same way we feel nasty after a big 2:00 am 5th meal at Taco Palace, these not-always-good news stories run through us and leave hell in its wake. Only, what's left behind in this case is more insidious than diarrhea.

Fear.

We learn from what's around us to be afraid of nearly everything.

Fear is why we work too long at jobs or careers that don't serve us. — fear of failure or poverty.

Fear is why we lie. — fear of being perceived as insignificant or unimportant.

Fear is why we act needy. — fear of not measuring up.

Fear is why we stay, when we know we should leave. — fear of the unknown.

Fear is why we blame the world outside for all the bad. — fear of having to deal with what's in our heads.

It's time we meet these tenants who we've we allowed to camp out in our mental houses and inspect the results of them taking up residence there.

Adrenaline Rush

There's instant reaction to hearing a horrific story, such as a family murdered, a child kidnapped, a suicide. It's like the train wreck you can't turn away from. After the initial shock — maybe a brief relief; "Thank God, it wasn't me."

In the Information Age it's easy to become hooked on the steady stream of stories and breaking news. Question is - after the storyline fades, what's being left behind?

With other adrenaline pumping activities, such as exercising, high-intensity sports or risky activities — you do the activity and right away, you're rewarded with a rush. With fear-inducing 'news' you get the rush; but you may not feel the often negative consequences until much later.

Leave it up to the media outlets we all know and love, to think about these things before they report these stories to us: "All press is good press" remember?

Let's say, by habit you might listen to news radio on your drive into work, hear local news updates through your friends or loved ones during the day, read magazine updates about the latest developing animal flu pandemic during your lunch break, tune in for the newest terrorist alert updates during the rush hour drive home and finally settle in for a nice evening of talking heads on the 8 o'clock evening slot.

See the pattern here?

So it stands to reason that when you finally do lie down for the night and begin to recap your day as your fall into a deep sleep; images of the day's news reports replay behind your closing eyes. What do those images look like? Maybe the characters in that last news story are now the children in your own family, your wife or sister — maybe even you, yourself. After a restless and shallow sleep you may wake up with these terrible thoughts swirling around in your mind. And what would any reasonable person do? Warn everyone of course. You may call and tell them all about the terrible things that are happening in the world and the things they should do to stay safe.

"Lock your house, lock your car, don't talk to strangers, keep your eyes down, keep your pocketbook close, don't share the elevator — don't trust your neighbors"…ad nauseum.

Now, don't get me wrong; these things do happen. Crimes *are* committed and people get hurt or killed. But have you ever, for a moment, honestly believed that we are designed to build our lives around the possibility of danger lurking around every corner? The answer is clearly, NO!

"…we are living in the information age where, on a daily basis, we are constantly exposed to an ever growing and rapidly changing pool of information. Being able to evaluate this information, sort the valuable from the trivial,

analyze its relevance and meaning, and relate it to other information is a priceless skill. Anyone who has studied the universe knows that there is no shortage of sources of energy in the universe, and that there is no shortage of energy sources on Earth. And yet, here we are, crawling on the surface of this dot we call Earth, extracting caloric content that's buried in the soil, and when you look at that, you can't help but reflect on how primitive that behavior is. "

-TEACHINGS OF REASON, Procer Khepri

It is a primitive reaction to be afraid. So, what is it that you're afraid of?

If you're thinking, "Well — everything", I understand. Thankfully, we don't have to *stay* afraid. Thankfully there is a way out.

The longer you ignore your fears, the more you let fear dominate your life. Instead, give your darkest fears a name and banish the fear from your mind forever. These fears always produce a 'crop' after their kind. If you are afraid you won't have enough — you'll penny pinch, and lose sight of opportunities right at your door. If you fear you'll get fired — you'll become suspicious and paranoid, losing sight of connections you might be able to make at the present job that will lead to a new job.

Cause/effect.

Naming your fear gives you power over it, your conquering it soon follows.

I am afraid of _____.
I am afraid that _____.
Thinking about _____scares me.

In an ideal world, the answers to all those questions would be "nothing".

You would be able to sleep by yourself in the dark, leap tall buildings in a single bound and ask for that raise you know you deserve without even breaking a sweat. For at least one of us, however, there are well-rehearsed fear scripts which stand in that little spot in your throat that gets tight when you think of what makes you afraid.

If nothing else — the answers to your 'I am afraid of" questions may just serve to light certain corners of our mind that have gone unnoticed for years. In these corners you'll find treasure you had long forgotten you possessed — you may perhaps even stumble upon your true name there between the dusty pages of doubt you thought were a good place for safekeeping such a thing.

Hey, now I recognize you!

I don't know what your parents named you, but around here, we call you:

Whole. Perfect. Strong. Powerful. Loving. Harmonious. Happy.

(Affirmation words of Charles F. Haanel, The Master Key System)

3: you don't have to be

"May we be fearless of friends and enemies...from known and unknown...from night and day...may all the directions be our allies."
– Atharva Veda

If we trace back through our family generations, we are sure to find examples of fearlessness. Maybe they were immigrants who left a familiar home country, former slaves, veterans of war and survivors of economic hardships, famine or persecution.

You are here because they were fearless.

You were born with the seeds of the same fearlessness.

But to be clear – fearlessness is not being completely free of fear; there is a difference between the healthy fear that acts as a human's early warning signal and the constant fear that forces us to lead a smaller life because we are too afraid to even try. No one will suggest you deny a healthy fear mechanism, at the same time we do not need to BE our fears.

Fearlessness simply means that we do not give fear the power.

Fearlessness can manifest in small ways, like courage. The courage that emerges at a moment's notice; when a blind man stumbles off the sidewalk curb of a busy street and you immediately move in to action - holding him back from crossing too soon.

Fearless is feeling afraid, and not denying it — acknowledging it, but never fleeing from it. We are not moved. We encounter our fear. We face it, examine it, measure its dimensions and name it. We move continuously closer to it until it disappears altogether and becomes just another part of the tapestry that is our life experience.

I'm sure you've heard the old adage, **"The only way out of it is through it."** Not only does fearlessness offer us the keys to the highest expression of ourselves, but it brings with it the strength to endure and persevere. A refusal to give in until the goal is accomplished.

Of all the things I wish for the most, I hope I can always hear this message rise within myself above the din of the crowd, above the hum of ticker tapes and news reels when I start to feel afraid — I wish to know that I *can* be afraid but I don't *have to* be afraid.

I have asked for the way to be revealed. And it has been. It will be revealed to you as well, if you ask.

"Increase in me that wisdom which discovers its truest interests."

Look at this fearless quality within you, this piece of your character that remains as yet underutilized. At this point, you just need to note that fearlessness is a quality you can attain — if you want it.

Start small.

Just say yes.

section ii.
you are the sun

1: a chi pet

"What you agree with, you give power to."

Would you agree with me, that it's amazing to breathe?

That deep long breath you take on a beach vacation or a lazy summer Sunday afternoon.

This luscious experience of breath stands in sharp contrast to the shallow, muted breaths we take while we're stuck in traffic or wringing our hands over calculating the monthly household budget. What's gives? Why can't we breathe like it's a Sunday afternoon all the time? We suffocate ourselves slowly, because we haven't learned how important it is not to.

In traditional Chinese culture, qì (also chi or ch'i) is the active principle forming part of any living thing. This active principle is what animates us and everything that lives. This power is power without direction, so that whatever you impress on it, you will get back in return.

"There is a real sun center in us, the Solar (or Sun) Plexus — that is awakened with proper breathing. This is a great nerve center situated back of the stomach. When this central Sun, from which all the nerves of the body radiate, is in its normal condition, it steadily radiates a real energy, just as the sun does. This energy vibrates through the nerve highways and by-ways of the body out toward the surface of the body in all directions (the mucous membranous surface, as well as the outer skin), and is thrown off in a real halo or atmosphere, which always envelopes the body. If this radiation from the Solar Plexus is positive enough, the influence of another person cannot disturb its steady, harmonious vibrations in the least."

–Just How to Wake The Solar Plexus, Elizabeth Towne

For some of us - our body energy has been much like an unruly pet that pisses all over the living room and just ate all the good shoes.

Good news.

We are the trainer.

Bad news.

We are the trainer.

You must make the first move. When you can approach fear with a calm-assertive energy: compassionate, but quietly in control – you will stop worrying over things that will probably never happen and only good will start to come together in your life.

'Good' here doesn't mean you'll be magically transported to a land of rainbows and unicorns (that's in the next book). 'Good' means you have learned to live within the continuous cycle of renewal and depletion.

"By acknowledging the highs but not depleting your energy in over-enthusiasm, you can handle the lows better when depression drains your energy levels. By emotionally detaching from all results by not over investing energy, or under-investing energy, you can walk the middle path in gratitude always and all ways. <u>In this way you can overcome the swings of the pendulum from highs to lows from lows to highs, and so on.</u>"

-How To Raise Your Vibration, Sabrina Reber

Now, I know the amount of decisions we already make in a day can make this exercise seem larger than life. Not only because we think around 60,000 thoughts per day but added to that is the steady barrage of influence in updates, newswires and statistical data meant to slant our view to one cause or another, one political party, product or team or another. Getting into the swing of things is no easy matter — but tormenting thoughts and chi gone awry must be set right immediately.

You are getting what your choices are asking for - the egg actually comes before the chicken.

Overindulgence in having your choices influenced has consequences. Some side effects of abdicating choice power; see: sleeping on your chi (energy, solar plexus):

Trusting gurus, celebrities and political leaders more than you trust yourself

Believing that other people will know how *you* should live

"People pleasing" in order to gain recognition

Blaming other people and outer circumstances for your 'misfortune'

Living the life society wants you to live, at the cost of your happiness

Comparing yourself to others

There are several ways to wake yourself and get that chi back in control. You energy is cultivated naturally through eating and sleeping. So that eating right and getting enough rest are the basic — first level — building blocks for balanced energy. You can continue to cultivate an active and balanced chi by meditation, internal alchemy or reiki.

Here are some basic exercises to try:

Exercise 1:

When you wake in the early morning - throw all windows and doors wide open; lie flat on your back in your bed with arms stretched out on either side of you and no pillow or covering.

Relax from head to foot; close your mouth; take a deep slow breath, filling the lungs evenly as possible all the way down; holding the breath as long as you can without straining and then seeing how very slowly and smoothly you can let the breath out.

Pay very particular attention to this. See how slowly and steadily you can exhale the breath.

Notice any tension or tightness in your muscles, jaw, stomach throat or face and release each point of tension in relaxation as you breathe.

Exercise 2:

Creating a 'ball' of energy.

Rub your hands together briskly.
This is the same motion you'd use to warm your hands on a cold day.

Hold the intention of feeling your chi or energy in your hands.

Be aware of your hands and feel for this life energy in each hand, feel the connection of energy between your two hands.

Pull your hands gently apart. After your hands feel warmth and you can feel the connection between your two hands, pull them apart gently and slowly.

Keep your hands and fingers soft. Let them flow smoothly through the air. Keep them relaxed and fluid.

Bring your hands closer together. When you feel the connection between your hands weaken, bring them back slowly together.

Don't let your hands touch.

To end this exercise, simply pull your hands slowly apart and let them drop down at your sides.

Exercise 3:

Pushing Water

Stand with your feet shoulder width apart. Hands with palms facing ground and fingertips pointing forward.

Slowly bring hands up to shoulder level. Imagine your hands bringing up water with them.

Now slowly push the water down.

Repeat steps 1-3 as desired.

Chi Maintenance

Start this with one day, or even half a day. Do this once a week. Later, as you get used to it, try a 2-3 day cleanse and see if you can work your way up to a week.

Let friends, family know that you're going to chill on email for a day (or few), you may not be available to answer. Especially ANYTHING IN ALL CAPS OR COLORED FONTS

Skip 'MURDER', 'KIDNAPPING', 'RAPE', 'TERRORIST' news articles

Ditch checking your favorite gossip blogs or celebrity news subscriptions

Unplug the TV and Internet (you'll live)

Set your car radio to classical music, jazz, religious, spiritual, world music or other non-verbal genres

Spend time creating, crafting, working on projects, getting outside, communicating with people in person, collaborating and exercising

Read books. Long essays or focus-positive articles you've been wanting to read — but haven't found the time to

Watch objective, thought-provoking films

Absolutely CUSTOMIZE this list, keeping in mind that the point of this cleanse is to purge all negative sources of information and increase the amount of positive, empowering activities and information.

Once you've made space for the new stuff to come in — take some time for this next step. Figuring out what to keep and what to throw away.

What are the most essential information streams you consume?

What can you cut out (or cut down on)?

Can you cut out half of what you currently consume, more?

You may want to reduce your intake to essentials only. For some of you that may mean 'People' magazine once a week — totally okay. **This is YOUR mental diet. Only you know what is going to work for you and what won't.**

This is not something you have to cheat at, not another regimented policy enforced by the pretend inner judge. This is for your benefit, and if reading a gossip rag every now and again makes you happy; by all means kick your feet up in your most comfy pink fuzzy slippers, pull out the tray of éclairs and go to town. Bliss is bliss, in whatever form that takes for you.

Just use your stream wisely, remembering that the goal is to cultivate fearlessness and balance your energy. When we engage in ways that judge or criticize others (gossip, tabloids, etc.); it tends to become easier to judge and criticize ourselves – as well, to think that we will be judged or criticized. So no one action goes out and returns void. Every action, every thought sends a ripple effect out into your life; bringing back to you its "equivalent harvest".

Feeding the Chi

Your fearlessness feeds on many combinations of traits familiar to you

COURAGE

ENDURANCE

HUMILITY

RECOGNIZING THE HIGHER THAN I

You reinforce and feed the fearless with like-minded friends, devotional, journaling, religious or spiritually-based literature, uplifting music, feel-good television shows, nature-based documentaries, etc.

Identify four or five people who can provide an encouraging and powerful word; keep these people on speed dial.

This group will become indispensable to you, for when you stumble and fall into a fearful trench — as you may, they will help you keep your mind focused.

A vital part of your training will involve learning the regenerative practices that keep you from becoming physically, spiritually or emotionally exhausted when you're working in fearlessness.

This includes:

How to protect yourself from absorbing negative energy

How to rejuvenate your own energy

How to avoid "compassion" fatigue

A useful rule of thumb is that if you spend a certain number of hours working in an especially toxic or negative, violent environment - you should spend as much as a quarter of that same amount of time doing regenerative practices to avoid negative effects.

You have it. You know it. Now use it.

2: rituals of a peaceful warrior

"If it is a battle you cannot win, don't fight."

The 20/80 Rule:

20% of the things in your life are bringing you 80% of the joy.

All of these little wars you think you have to choose between, you don't.

After a while, the chi obedience training won't seem so daunting. It will be easy like Sunday morning. Don't get me wrong, it _is_ a choice you consciously and continually must make, but after repetition it becomes like breathing (again).

So - thank the job where you had to work twice as hard, to come away with only half the recognition. It made you better. Bless the parents that gave what they did. Good, bad. They steered you towards your destiny. Make peace with the abuse, the violation and the shadow, the obsession and compulsion, the contradiction and the ruse.

These are all actually your tools and they have always been yours to use. You gave away your power to these tools and expected them to build you a strong house — on their own. They could not. Take yourself back, and stand aright. You are the builder.

Now, if you've fed and trained the chi from the last section, you are ready to begin the rituals of a peaceful warrior — preparing the way. The peaceful warrior combines both courage and love, a warrior's spirit with a peaceful heart.

These rituals are where we go when we need to rest or let the 'wars' play out. These rituals are how we take out the trash and clear our mind of everything we don't need.

Use liberally:

- Exercise
- Team Sports
- Hot Baths
- Meditation Music
- Sitting Silently

After some practice, we won't need to physically transport ourselves there. We will carry 'there' with us.

Can you remember the last time you engaged in one of these rituals, how great you felt after? How about the first time you spoke up in a situation you normally wouldn't; the hot/cold rush to your face and the light on your feet almost prancing (pranic-being) feeling.

In the hopes that you read this and said, "Yeah — well, I already speak up for myself and I'm not into the walk-all-over-me way of living. That's what this sounds like." I hear you. And this is not that way.

The warrior listens. The warrior fights when there is a true need aroused. The warrior uses energy wisely. Conserves. Targets. Strikes.

There is treasure inside of you, in need of your agreement to protect it. In this way, the warrior must fight. There is a light inside of you that must shine, it is for this you must fight.

You've trained it, fed it and now know how to direct the light of your chi to show you the way of fearlessness and the bringing forward of your day.

"Meditate. Eat Right. Pray First. Then Fight."
–Saul Williams s√he

3: but you already knew that

"Intuition is a spiritual faculty it does not explain, it merely points the way."

—Florence Scovel Shinn, New Thought Teacher

In section i, you remembered who you were and heard your true name again for the first time. You chose not to be afraid anymore and learned how fear exists only by your choice. In section ii, you started to become the sun again and get your chi in check.

But none of this is any surprise because you already knew all that stuff.

You already knew that when you came into this world, you came from something greater than yourself – the core of which you still carry inside of you. You already knew that as an Earth astronaut, anything on top of breezing through space on a water rock is icing on the proverbial cake.

Right?

You already knew that this giant animal kingdom we live in has us smack on top, not because we have thumbs — but because we are conscious of the truth that all is connected.

Before you picked up this book - you already knew that if, for 30 minutes a day, you sat perfectly still and breathed perfectly deeply — you'd change the way you see everything. That if you rode a bike, or ran or flew, or rowed or sweat until your heart pumped double time; clean, oxygenated blood would flow throughout your body — refreshing the whole system and giving you the clear focus to make good choices.

You knew all that because it's you and if you know anything — you know yourself.

Right?

It may seem counterintuitive to have to learn yourself. Surely that should be a given.

Not necessarily.

Sometimes we tend to live 'around' the real us, like a little child's game of duck-duck-goose.

As Christopher Alexander observed: **"It is hard, so terribly hard, to please yourself. Far from being**

the easy thing that it sounds like, it is almost the hardest thing in the world, because we are not always comfortable with that true self that lies deep within us."

You do *not* get to know yourself simply by growing up and growing old. Knowing yourself is a conscious effort; you do it with intention and purpose. Knowing yourself doesn't happen at once. It's what we are all doing, every moment. You might remember Malcolm Gladwell's 10,000 hours rule. The rule is, in order for you to be an expert on a subject, you first need to put in 10,000 hours of practice (about five years).

10,000 hours to know yourself – Go.

"Man's work is only with himself. When he changes, everything changes."

Personally observing and experiencing the reality of which you are a part is one method for starting the self-discovery conversation.

Get-To-Know-You:

Bless the past and forget it. Bless the future and know it has endless joys in store for you.

Think about the concept and the science of the Universe.

Think about planet Earth, and its relation to the Universe.

Think about the existence of your biological parents in relation to your personal existence.

Think about what you need for your personal survival.

Examine the relationship between your body and mind and the continual interaction between them.

Think about the significance of your physical senses and reflexes.

Enjoy the power and freedom of making personal decisions.

Study your amazing abilities as a sentient member of the human race.

Accept your innate desire for superiority, it's natural – we all feel it.

Examine your natural curiosity about reality.

Pay Intuition Attention

Daily decisions throughout the day are made very quickly and easily by relying on habit. Things like: deciding to wash my face and brush my teeth first thing in the morning.

Bigger decisions rely on analytical process where we sort out and weigh practical concerns, consequences, how we feel about the situation, and responses of friends, family or those affected by the decision.

When we more regularly engage in (chi training) meditation or other spiritual exercises which quiet the mind and reactive impulses, there may be a small voice that starts pushing in a particular direction, which we "know" (or feel or sense) is what we "should" do—the "right" decision. Some people have called this the 'The Conscience' or The Holy Spirit'.

Sometimes the urge is different from what we would normally have chosen to do. This "urge"—or what people might refer to as 'an inner voice' is what the word 'intuition' refers to.

Now, in the same way the windshield of a car or the lens of a camera can become obscured by the haze and dirt from everyday use – our intuitive faculties (knowing from inside) can be broken and sullied from ignorance and misuse. You won't recognize your own intuition without self-knowledge. But this 'gut feeling' is critical to the fear-less process as it is your own surefire global positioning system. Listen to it, heed it, trust it and reinforce it by its regular use.

One of these days soon, you'll write down the most difficult thing you can think of. Allowing yourself to write exactly what you <u>don't</u> want to write about, seeing what needs to be worked out come onto that page.

That's the day you'll know that you've found exactly where to go when you have questions about yourself and your life experiences. Within.

To the teacher within, who will not explain but simply point the way.

section iii.
if you choose

1: stop

"fear is much easier to deal with when you know exactly what it is you're afraid of, and <u>why</u> are you afraid of what you're afraid of?"

Are you afraid of homelessness, lack of options, shame, embarrassment, or loss of meaning in life? Are you afraid of losing your house, being unqualified for a job, what your spouse may think, being embarrassed in front of your friends?

These are all legitimate fears.

But these are all also things you can get some control over and just coming to terms with that can take a lot of fear's power away. You might feel a real sense of personal power return to you after realizing what you're actually afraid of.

Sometimes this helps. If it does, you win, and the day is saved. But for some fears you're just getting started.

Follow those fears back to their origination.

Go through each step of what happens if your worst possible fear were to come true?

"I'm afraid I'll end up homeless" is a vague, out-of-your-control fear that will keep you in a blind panic.

And even then, homeless people have been known to turn into great successes: Halle Berry, Jim Carrey, Suze Orman, Daniel Craig and most famously — Chris Gardner subject of the movie starring Will Smith, "The Pursuit of Happyness."

"I'm afraid he'll fall in love with someone else"

There is no shortage of 'fish in the sea' (7 Billion at last count) and you cannot be separated from the true love and companionship which is yours by right. You may need to let go of the pictures in your head of you think it should be, but you will have what is made for you.

"I'm afraid I won't find another job"

Out of your control?

In the age of information, where a good person like you is able to read something like this — is a marketplace where a good person like you can do pretty much anything you could dream of, and do well at it. I mean, a kid sold a million pixels for $1 each and become a millionaire — anything is still possible for you.

Are you sure of what you're really afraid of?

"Our deepest fear is not that we are inadequate. Our deepest fear is that we are powerful beyond measure. It is our light, not our darkness that most frightens us. We ask ourselves, 'Who am I to be brilliant, gorgeous, talented and fabulous?' Actually, who are you not to be? You are a child of God. **Your playing small does not serve the world.** There is nothing enlightened about shrinking so that other people won't feel insecure around you. **We are all meant to shine, as children do.** We were born to make manifest the glory of God that is within us. It's not just in some of us; it's in everyone. And as we let our own light shine, we unconsciously give other people permission to do the same. **As we are liberated from our own fear, our presence automatically liberates others."**
— Marianne Williamson, Return to Love: Reflections on the Principles of "A Course in Miracles"

I know that when you're in the middle of it, when your throat is tight and your jaw is tensed – I know. It's most certainly not imaginary – as we all know – there are real psychological and physiological impacts of being afraid.

But in that moment...

Stop.

Remind yourself.

Put the fear down for a quick second.

Stand still or sing, dance, pray, make music, run or bike.

Ring the bells and clap the cymbals and dissolve that fear right down to a grain of sand. The goal here is to get out of the fear rut as quickly as you can and come immediately into the recognition of your power and your Source.

Where do your beliefs live, in the avalanche of supplies or the lack of things? **"No man can serve two masters."** Make room for the right version of a thing, to come take the place of whatever has been outgrown and is causing you pains - fear. You will remain wherever you are until you can see through where you are. Only then, will you move peacefully into the next state of learning and experiencing. If you can approach things with that knowledge, then whatever is not made of truth will simply dissolve away.

Stunt Doubles

Fear likes to wear disguises and call itself by different names: resentment, anxiety, dependence, gossip…

When confronted with any of these, make the builder's statement:

"I put this (worry, burden, lack) down and am free of it."

Where you "put it down" may depend on your personal sources. If you understand religion, you may say "I give my burden to God, Jesus or The Holy Spirit". If you understand scientific principles, you may say "I will give this problem over to my subconscious mind to figure out a solution." Whatever the raw material is that you work with; the law which governs the weight of mental things is the same. "What you agree with, you give power to."

We must speak to ourselves in this manner. We must address ourselves with spoken words. This is our life.

This is our kingdom. Be steady and your vision will clear.

Finally.

Perfect health, wealth, love and self-actualization.

Finally.

Peace. Power. Plenty.

In the end, fear is only energy being misdirected. Our task is to change it into something else like surrender, believing or wisdom, a lesson; ever building a bridge to the peace and happiness of our life. That's the real secret of personal power.

Break free of the life that's built around fear and walk head first into the life you long for.

How do I get rid of fear right now?

- Surrender
- Therapy
- Journaling
- Breathing
- Prayer
- Perspective

2: caution (is not fear)

"There is no conflict between confidence and caution."

— The Discourses of Epictetus

Wherever you're standing right now, let's just for arguments' sake say that you're actually in a State Park camping outside under a hand-made teepee with your three small children. And let's also say that it is 'bear season' - if there can be such a thing in a forest.

In a hypothetical, but very actual, event you would probably be fairly terrified that during the night you may end up tomorrow's news headline.

Perfectly rational on your part.

Thankfully, we came with that warning detection system. This would tell us that the teepee episode – was not the smartest thing we've ever done, and never will again. Caution – meet the reader. Reader – meet caution. Shake hands, make nice. Caution is why we apply the brake as we come upon a traffic light, caution is why we drive more slowly through a neighborhood where small kids may be playing, caution is we hunch over when walking under a low ceiling: a care taken to avoid danger.

However; nebulous fear about the past, present or future is not caution and must be eradicated completely and immediately.

The power of discernment is in knowing when to say 'yes' to this caution and when to say 'no'. The ability to judge situations well is a friend to us and we should be thankful for it. When it becomes a discipline, you open up a spot for information that you didn't know before and more information can only improve the framework for making decisions. **We know caution because it is not the crippling mental attitude of fearfulness; it is the announcement of a clear choice to avoid outcomes we do not want.**

Fear is like an out of tune key on a piano that you can track back to a core belief which causes you to feel the fear (out of tune). Change the tone of the key (fine tuning) so the new belief is tuned into harmony with the rest of your life. Let us apply more awareness to our choices, let's work towards less reaction.

Caution, and then continue. Decide then act.

Fear is caution gone awry with paralyzing effects. Careful planning and not fear will help you in whatever outcome you are trying to make. In my experience, fear can disguise itself as something practical yet it has brought many to a permanent state of standstill.

You may be so used to these daily patterns that you don't realize how cumulatively harmful they can be, and you can - without realizing it - allow yourself to be taken by this fear. If there is one secret to this understanding then it is that there is something larger than yourself which has already proven willing to share the burden. Use it.

You won't become an expert at this overnight — you will become an expert over time.

Be careful how you talk to yourself about what you fear.

And then, try this: Instead of first thinking about the worst case scenario, try imagining the best.

Know that you don't have to overcome your fear all at once.

And then, try this: Go back to your list of things you're afraid of. Make a list of one step you can take to start facing each fear. Take that step.

Realize that everyone is afraid of something.

And then, try this: Find someone to talk to about your fears — you may discover that they have found a way through those fears and can help you too.

Look at fears as avenues for you to grow.

And then, try this: Talk to yourself about how things would be different if you overcame your fear.

3: go

"Do it."

At this very moment, if you are on the same planet as I am, you are sitting on a large water covered rock which is floating through space at a speed of 460 meters per second--or roughly 1,000 miles per hour.

In addition, our solar system--Earth and all--whirls around the center of our galaxy at some 220 kilometers per second, or 490,000 miles per hour. –
How Fast Is The Earth Moving, Scientific American, October 2012

490,000 miles per hour?!

Pretty scary, huh?

And yet, this morning we all woke up like it was just another day.

Interesting.

Even as you read this now, you are breathing in a delicate balance of Oxygen, Nitrogen, Argon and small amounts of other gases. Again, no one is stopping me on the street and wondering whether their next breath will contain the right balance of each to keep them alive.

It's not that we don't recognize the delicate nature of the earth's marvelous demonstrations. **It's that we trust in it all working out and working perfectly — we just breathe.**

It really is that simple.

This may be single most important thing you can believe for yourself and others. Fearlessness is contagious, so that doing this for yourself gives the rest of us permission to be BRAVE and feel afraid but to do it anyway!

In 2011, I left a job I was unhappy with and took a risk, (kids and all)! Packed everything I owned into my car and drove halfway across the country to strike it out as an independent consultant - I had no idea what consulting meant, let alone how to make money doing it! I only knew two things:

1. I had never before been without anything I needed. Whether from the kindness of strangers, or by pure miracle - there was never a true need that wasn't met.

2. That if I succeeded or failed, it would be my own and it was better than spending 8 hours a day, for almost five years being miserable and counting the days until the next weekend rolled around.

I jumped and by grace, the net appeared.

Now, the story doesn't end "she lived happily ever after with all the consulting work she could handle"...but it was never meant to.

She did live HAPPILY, thereafter though. Now doing what she loves, influencing people and policy, using what she's good at to be the boss she never had, pushing the next generation of leaders to believe in themselves and others!

When I come back from vacation, I can't wait to get back to work, because it isn't work. It's what I love. It's what I chose and continue to choose every day, and the day I wake up to find this isn't what I want to do anymore. I won't.

I was lucky enough to have women (and men) in my life who went before me and showed me that the gap between here and there is smaller than it appears, so I pay it forward and only tell you that's it IS all possible. All you have to do is decide, surrender and trust. There's light on the path. Pick your head up. Fix your eyes. It's all already yours.

Go get it.

I woke up one day wanting to know present, actual freedom. How to feel at peace when my heart is racing in anger over something she said, or he did, or they wanted. How to be calm when a bank account was getting low. How to think "yes" when people were telling me "no".

I wanted to learn more than just how to live, I wanted to learn how to be alive! The more I learned, the less I hung on to the movements outside of me. If this desire of yours is sufficiently strong, it will carry you.

And before I forget to tell you: people <u>will</u> THINK things. Believe me.

At some point in my life, someone has thought — or will think - I'm a bad parent, daughter, sister or friend.

Or people will say "Nira is a fake". Or people will say "her writing is so crazy, or over the top" whatever that means. Or they will say "she just pretends it's all sunshine and butterflies" or people will think "she's making herself look like a jackass". They'll say "she's so naïve and arrogant".

So what.

They'll say these things and sometimes they'll be wrong — but sometimes, they'll be 100% right. What you must realize is that you can say, "Okay" to these things without letting the fear of opinions; take you off track. We can say "Okay" to these things and then listen for the lesson between what's being said while we KEEP MOVING ONE FOOT IN FRONT OF THE OTHER. **These things have no power to harm you — if you do not give them the power to. Period.**

"Love your enemies, bless them that curse you. Do good to them that hate you. Pray for them which spitefully use you and persecute you." -FSS

Maybe the lesson is you've allowed unhealthy people into your life to fix, or repair or save them — you cannot. It's also possible that the lesson is you need to check yourself — do it. Part of the 'fearless' package is being squarely responsible for how you see the world and how you act towards it.

Reading about fearlessness will not bring it into your mind. Work is necessary. Hard mental labor is the most important step.

Can you do all of this?

Yes.

The best way to find the yellow brick road of your life is to start out where you are standing now. Become so preoccupied in making the best of it, having fun, and challenging yourself that you stop thinking about the path. One day, not so long from now, you'll notice that you're walking on 24 karats. And you'll wonder just when that transformation actually took place.

Go.

Now.

power manifesto

In this life, there are two kinds of beings…

There are victims, and things happen to them.

And there are creators, who create as they observe.

At the deepest level, we are all one thing. Molecules, atoms, energy.

There is no separation, as drops of water make an ocean.

All we have ever experienced has lived inside the visual cortex of the brain. The outward projection is a series of optical illusions.

Our sense of touch is an electrical impulse...a set of instructions for the brain to decode.

You are existing right now the way you see yourself in your mind.

These words you are reading are in your brain, as every sight, every sound, every texture, every smell... but it goes deeper.

Everything is only your projection of it.

i.7 : six impossible things before breakfast

"I'm just one hundred and one, five months and a day."

"I can't believe that!" said Alice.

"Can't you?" the Queen said in a pitying tone. **"Try again: draw a long breath, and shut your eyes."**

Alice laughed. "There's no use trying," she said: "one can't believe impossible things."

"I daresay you haven't had much practice," said the Queen. "When I was your age, I always did it for half-an-hour a day. Why, sometimes I've believed as many as six impossible things before breakfast."

-Through the Looking-Glass, Lewis Carroll

about the author:

Nira Minniefield was born in the Hudson Valley Region of New York and has been breaking the 'rules' since 1979.

mom to three guaranteed game changers.

information solutions provider and founder of twelve oak consulting.

contributing travel & food writer at Liberator Magazine, a publication known for its cutting edge take on 'art. culture. education. politics. truth...' her articles include: 'A Funny thing Happened on the Way to the Pharmacy' offering a glimpse into the evolution of lifestyle. You'll find her blog at talesfromearth.tumblr.com

aspiring food curator (she made that up around the same time she made up the term 'flexitarian') whose love for natural, real foods led to the 2009 opening of a natural foods café and an all-natural kids lunch service in Baltimore, MD. She blogs about her recipes, theories on life and mommy musings at lunchbynature.wordpress.com

New York native who considers Toronto, South Korea and Marrakech all hometowns — she has established a secret HQ somewhere near Annapolis, MD where you might find her crossing off the next #40before40 and planning a 'Round-The-World' un-school adventure with her children.

14696828R00042

Printed in Great Britain
by Amazon.co.uk, Ltd.,
Marston Gate.